Amaryllis

& Little Witch

Amaryllis & Little Witch

by *Pascal Brullemans*
translated by *Alexis Diamond*

Playwrights Canada Press
Toronto

LIBRARY AND ARCHIVES CANADA CATALOGUING IN PUBLICATION
Title: Amaryllis ; & Little witch / by Pascal Brullemans ; translated by Alexis Diamond.
Other titles: Plays. Selections. English | Little witch
Names: Brullemans, Pascal, 1971- author. | Diamond, Alexis (Playwright), translator. | container of (expression): Brullemans, Pascal, 1971- Vipérine. English. | container of (expression): Brullemans, Pascal, 1971- Petite sorcière. English.
Description: Two plays. | Translations of: Vipérine and Petite sorcière
Identifiers: Canadiana (print) 20200252607 | Canadiana (ebook) 20200252747 | ISBN 9780369101143 (softcover) | ISBN 9780369101150 (PDF) | ISBN 9780369101167 (EPUB) | ISBN 9780369101174 (Kindle)
Classification: LCC PS8603.R844 A2 2020 | DDC C842/.6—dc23

Playwrights Canada Press operates on Mississaugas of the Credit, Wendat, Anishinaabe, Métis, and Haudenosaunee land. It always was and always will be Indigenous land.

We acknowledge the financial support of the Canada Council for the Arts—which last year invested $153 million to bring the arts to Canadians throughout the country—the Ontario Arts Council (OAC), Ontario Creates, and the Government of Canada for our publishing activities.

To Pascal Brullemans,
friend and kindred
spirit.
—AD

Amaryllis

To my daughters.

——PB

Translator's Foreword

As an anglophone theatre artist in Québec, what draws me to contemporary Québec French is that it was forged in the theatre, and it is in the theatre that it continues to ferment and foment, grow and bloom. Anchored in a place and a people, it is beautiful to behold for its richness, uniqueness, and rarity. Each playwright in turn claims it, shapes it, prunes it, transplants it, marking it as their very own. It is a living, surging thing, a force of nature, and its soil is the stage.

This is also why being an anglophone theatre artist in Québec feels like such an anomaly. Because English is everywhere, all around, belonging to everyone and to no one. English may well be the vehicle for anglophone theatre, but it is not its *raison d'être*.

The seeds of my involvement in Québécois theatre were planted around the time I first met Pascal Brullemans, entirely by chance. Despite our different mother tongues, we spoke the same language, and I discovered in Pascal a kindred spirit. Then, as often happens, we lost touch.

Years later, Playwrights' Workshop Montréal (PWM) announced their first ever translation unit to train a new generation of theatre translators. I wanted to apply, but I needed a Québécois play to translate.

So one day I was at PWM, discussing the situation with artistic director Emma Tibaldo, when Fate (also known as dramaturgy) intervened by way of an email. Jessie Mill, coordinator of international activities at CEAD (Centre des auteurs/ autrices dramatiques), had a script that was a real *coup de coeur* (an untranslatable term meaning that she loved it), and she was looking for a translator. The author was none other than Pascal Brullemans.

I began to read, and by the end of the opening monologue in *Vipérine* (a.k.a. *Amaryllis*), I was weeping at the beauty and the depth and the humanity and the humour; a *coup de coeur*, indeed.

But that was just the beginning.

Translator's Note on the Title

Vipérine = a flowering plant that grows in inhospitable soil whose stem is scaly like a viper's skin; in English, it is called "the pride of Madeira."

Amaryllis = a flowering plant and member of the poisonous belladonna family. While the bulb is ugly, the bloom is beautiful.

Vipérine was first produced by Maison de la culture Maisonneuve, Montréal, in 2012 with the following cast and creative team:

Marilyn Perreault
Léonie Saint-Onge
Sébastien Rajotte
Michel Mangeau

Director: Nini Belanger
Assistant Director: Andrée-Anne Garneau
Set Design: Julie Vallée-Léger
Costume Design: Geneviève Bouchard
Technical Director: Charles Maher
Lighting Design: David-Alexandre Chabot
Sound Design: Michel F. Côté

The translation was initially developed at the 2011 Playwrights' Workshop Montréal Translation Unit with unit dramaturg Maureen Labonté. Subsequently, Maureen provided dramaturgical support through Playwrights' Workshop Montréal with a grant from Emploi Québec.

The translation was further developed with the support of the 2016 Glassco Translation Residency in Tadoussac through Playwrights' Workshop Montréal with residency dramaturg Bobby Theodore.

In October 2016, with support from the Canada Council for the Arts, Toronto's Theatre Direct hosted a two-day workshop and a public reading of *Amaryllis* in the Wychwood Theatre, led by Lynda Hill and featuring Bria McLaughlin as Amaryllis, Martin Julien as the Narrator, Lucy Hill as Fey, and Jeff Yung as Dad.

Dramatis Personae

Amaryllis, ten years old
Fey, nine years old
Dad, forty years old
and the Narrator, ageless

1.

The NARRATOR enters.

NARRATOR

When Amaryllis's dad got the call, he was already close to the breaking point, and what he was about to hear would only make it worse. You see, her dad's life basically revolved around work. Not because he loved money, or because he was ambitious, but because only work felt real. Eat, drive, work, sleep, over and over again. That's pretty much all he could do to fill the emptiness inside him. When Amaryllis's dad got the call, he'd been living with this emptiness for three years. It showed up after the death of his first child. Her absence left a gaping hole that had to be filled. Especially when another little girl, very much alive, was waiting to play in the park, chase creepy-crawlies, and eat candy. Unfortunately, her dad didn't have the heart for any of this, as if Death had killed all joy the instant It claimed his first child. When the office called with condolences and asked, flat out, when he thought he might come back to work, Amaryllis's dad answered, "How about right now." You see, when her dad was at work, he felt in control, making it a lot easier to forget about the emptiness. Her mother couldn't bear it and left. So, when the phone rang, her dad was on his way to a meeting. He grabbed the phone, annoyed by the new ring tone Amaryllis had downloaded.

DAD enters. The phone rings.

DAD
Hello?

NARRATOR
There was that nasal voice he knew all too well. He was tempted to hang up, to disappear . . . but he didn't.

"Good morning, Mr. Gray. This is the principal speaking."

DAD
Let me stop you right there. I know what you're going to say. But today's her birthday, so you can tell her that if she doesn't behave, she can kiss her party, her cake, and her presents goodbye!

NARRATOR
"I'm afraid that won't be possible, sir."

DAD
Why not?

NARRATOR
"She ran away."

DAD
What????!!!!

NARRATOR
"She told her friends she had a mission and left."

DAD
When did this happen?

NARRATOR
"At recess."

DAD
What about the recess monitor?

NARRATOR
"We're terribly sorry."

DAD
Sorry won't bring her back!

NARRATOR
"Has she called you?"

DAD
What do you think?

NARRATOR
"Is there someone else she might've contacted?"

DAD
Her mother's away until the end of the month.

NARRATOR
"Then we'll have to notify the police."

DAD
The police?

NARRATOR
"They'll head up the search."

DAD
The search . . .

NARRATOR
"I'll call you as soon as I hear anything."

DAD
Wait . . . !

DAD hangs up and then runs off.

2.

AMARYLLIS enters lugging her knapsack.

NARRATOR
Meanwhile, on the other side of town, Amaryllis was walking down to the pier all by herself. It was her birthday, normally a cause for celebration. But that morning she'd woken up with a heavy heart and one thing on her mind . . .

AMARYLLIS
It's not a thing, it's a mission!

NARRATOR
Right, right . . . which is why she left school and headed down to the river . . .

AMARYLLIS
Okay, back off.

NARRATOR
Excuse me . . . ?

AMARYLLIS
I'm not in the mood.

NARRATOR
Don't you want me to tell these people your story?

AMARYLLIS
It's none of their beeswax.

NARRATOR
They might want to know what'll happen to you.

AMARYLLIS
I'm not so special.

NARRATOR
How do you know? You might be.

AMARYLLIS
Too late.

NARRATOR
Too late for what?

AMARYLLIS
She already beat me to it.

NARRATOR
What do you mean?

AMARYLLIS

I mean Super Sister already took the job. She went through hell at the hospital while I was watching Disney movies on the couch with my babysitter, waiting for everyone to come home.

NARRATOR

And they did.

AMARYLLIS

Not everyone. Just my parents. One night they came home white as sheets. And the way they held me in their arms, I just knew that was it. Game over.

NARRATOR

She might be gone, but you're still here.

AMARYLLIS

What can I do to top being dead? She was so beautiful, so brave, so, so everything, I can't compete. She was the sun, and I'm Pluto!

NARRATOR

Sorry, but since you're the only one here, yours is the story I have to tell.

AMARYLLIS

That's where you're wrong.

NARRATOR

Who else is there?

AMARYLLIS
Lemme show you. In my knapsack.

AMARYLLIS takes out the urn.

AMARYLLIS
Ta-da!

NARRATOR
Your sister's urn?

AMARYLLIS
Her ashes are in it.

NARRATOR
Why do you have the urn in your bag?

AMARYLLIS
None of your beeswax.

NARRATOR
Look, I'm not here to tell a story about a can.

AMARYLLIS
I told you it's too late. Nobody ever listens to me!

NARRATOR
There must be another way.

AMARYLLIS
How about leaving me alone?

NARRATOR
The story would be too short.

AMARYLLIS
Great! Can I go now?

NARRATOR
Do you think about her once in a while?

AMARYLLIS
How could I forget? My sister's still here, even though she's dead.

A young girl enters dressed like a princess.

FEY
Hello.

AMARYLLIS
What did I tell you?

NARRATOR
She's very pretty.

AMARYLLIS
She's perfect.

NARRATOR
What's her name?

FEY

Blessed by my parents' choice
—aptly named, I rejoice—
lucky me, what can I say?
Please feel free to call me Fey.

NARRATOR

You've mastered the art of rhyme.

FEY

It sounds much more refined.

NARRATOR

It's quite rare these days, I agree.

FEY

May we be introduced formally—?

NARRATOR

I'm the one telling the story.

FEY

Have we met previously—?
Your voice bestirs a memory—

NARRATOR

It's in the realm of possibility.

AMARYLLIS

Okay, you two dictionaries. Put a sock in it. A narrator and a
heroine, that's like peanut butter and chocolate, a match made
in heaven! So why don't you go tell each other stories someplace
else. Go on, get out of here . . .

FEY

But sweet sister mine . . .

AMARYLLIS

You can thank me later.

FEY

I'm staying, sister mine,
to protect you from danger.
I won't leave you behind
to run off with a stranger.

AMARYLLIS

He's not a stranger, just a voice.

FEY

What if I were to say
that voice fills me with dismay.
But first tell me without delay:
Why are you on the pier?
Is school done for the day?
Do the adults know you're here?

AMARYLLIS

What are you, the police?

FEY

Still that permanent pout
when you disobey?
When Mom and Dad find out
you will surely pay.

AMARYLLIS

Sometimes you gotta do what you gotta do.
I'm on a mission.

FEY

A mission? But for whom?
Do you dare to presume
you can save the orphaned
and the sick from certain doom?

AMARYLLIS

I can't say. It's personal.

FEY

A secret wrong to set right?
Need my help and advice?
Our duo could reunite
to end your quest in a trice!

AMARYLLIS

It's okay. I'll do it myself.

FEY

Just put me to the test.
Let me join in your quest—
I beg you, please, say yes!

AMARYLLIS
Whoa! You're like sticky glue.

NARRATOR
Ah. Now I understand.

AMARYLLIS
What?

NARRATOR
You stole the urn for your mission.

FEY
What's this I hear?

AMARYLLIS
Thought I told you to back off!

FEY
Did I hear correctly?
You kidnapped me?

AMARYLLIS
It's not kidnapping if you're already dead.

FEY
What shall we call it instead?

NARRATOR
Desecration, maybe.

FEY

You profaned my remains?
You should be ashamed!

AMARYLLIS

I didn't do anything wrong, okay!

FEY

And now you add a lie
to your other crimes—!

AMARYLLIS

Calm down!

FEY

You have no alibi—
These are evil times!

AMARYLLIS

Don't move!

FEY

Give me that urn, traitor,
or I will lose my temper.

AMARYLLIS

One more step and I'll dump your ashes on this pile of
doggie doo.

FEY

You'd befoul me so?
You wouldn't . . . would you?

AMARYLLIS
Want to find out?

FEY
It's inconceivable
a bloodline so noble
could be thus defiled
by a creature so vile.

AMARYLLIS
You got all the good stuff. That left all the bad for me.

FEY
Cursèd be she
who betrays her family!

AMARYLLIS
Oh, yeah? What if I don't have a family no more!

FEY
"What if I *haven't* got a family *any*more . . . "

AMARYLLIS
What?

FEY
You used a double negative.

AMARYLLIS
How can you be so perfect and not get it!

FEY

What have I failed to grasp?

AMARYLLIS

How everything got messed up when you left! Mom took off.
Dad's been a total zombie. The only time they're kinda with it
is when they're standing in front of the mantelpiece looking at
your urn.

FEY

You can't just steal my urn,
a gesture most unwise!
It won't undo the turn
of my untimely demise.

AMARYLLIS

It's all I could come up with.

FEY

So, what is your plan for my ashes?

AMARYLLIS

I was just going to throw you off the end of the pier.

FEY

You wish to drown the dead?

AMARYLLIS

Well . . . maybe it's not the best idea.

FEY

It's absurd!

AMARYLLIS
You got a better one?

FEY
Yes! Seek assistance!

AMARYLLIS
Watch Miss Perfect fall apart.

FEY
I'd rather be perfect
than wicked!

AMARYLLIS
I'd rather be wicked
than dead!

FEY
Enough, please stop.
You've gone too far.
Think being dead
is fun—a lark?
I didn't want
to fade away,
nor do I want
to stay this way.

AMARYLLIS
So why are you here?

FEY

I'm hanging on by a thread.
Once dead, my relieved soul fled,
crossed over to the other side,
where I met sad souls who tried
so desperately to find a door.
I found mine but could do no more,
held back by a bit of ribbon.
I traced it here, to its origin,
my last earthly tie drawing me
to the foot of the white tree.

NARRATOR

At the centre of the garden stands the Ribbon Tree. It is what is
holding your sister back. Thousands of ribbons are tangled in
its branches. One thread for each of the dead whose loved ones
refuse to let go.

AMARYLLIS

Why didn't you untie yourself?

FEY

No solution availed.
Whatever I tried, failed.

NARRATOR

Only the living can untie the knots.

AMARYLLIS

Well, if that's all, I'll go do it.

NARRATOR

You can't just enter the Land of the Dead like it's the mall.

FEY

I could be your guide,
but promise to be good—
don't make me nag or chide.
Swear to listen as you should!

AMARYLLIS

On one condition.

FEY

State your terms.

AMARYLLIS

No more rhymes. That's it. I'm fed up. Starting now, you talk like everybody else.

FEY

You demand too high a price
for so great a sacrifice!

AMARYLLIS

Fine. Whatever.

FEY

Wait! Okay . . . I'll try.

AMARYLLIS

Deal! So, which way to the Land of the Dead?

FEY
To cross to the other side,
simply swallow your pride,
promise this hand to heed
wherever it shall lead.

AMARYLLIS
I'm sorry, what was that?

FEY
Hold my hand.

AMARYLLIS
Now you're talking.

    FEY takes her sister's hand.

AMARYLLIS
Brrr . . . Your hand is cold.

FEY
Welcome to the Land of the Dead.

AMARYLLIS
Awesome.

    The NARRATOR picks up the thread of the story, but his voice
    grows softer and softer, until it's no longer audible.

NARRATOR
That's how the sisters crossed the border between the living and the dead. They walked until they came to the outskirts of the Valley of Shadows, the first stop on their mini odyssey . . ..

AMARYLLIS
I don't hear the narrator anymore.

FEY
He can't follow us. What happens here can't be described.

AMARYLLIS
It's getting pretty dark.

FEY
I know where I'm going.

AMARYLLIS
I'm glad I'm not alone.

FEY
We haven't played together in a long time.

AMARYLLIS
Maybe because I don't need you as much anymore.

FEY
Don't be silly. Everyone needs a big sister.
How many times did I protect you from the monsters under the bed, or when the other kids were mean to you?

Do you remember all our grand adventures whenever we left the house? Okay, sure, sometimes they didn't turn out so well, but we always had fun.

AMARYLLIS
Fey . . .

FEY
What?

AMARYLLIS
The colours . . . It's like they disappeared.

FEY
Totally normal. We're in the Valley of Shadows. Keep walking.

AMARYLLIS *(looking at the flowers of the Valley)*
I can't imagine how anything can grow here.

FEY
Come on, keep moving.

AMARYLLIS *(trying to pick the flowers)*
Look, they just fall apart. Like ashes.

FEY
This landscape is an imitation.

AMARYLLIS
Super weird.

FEY

We can't stay here.

AMARYLLIS

Why?

FEY

Because he'll find you.

AMARYLLIS

Who?

FEY

The dog with three heads.

AMARYLLIS

You mean like a huge, scary dog that drools and everything?

FEY

His job is to keep the living from entering the garden. So if the first head sees you, you drop dead on the spot. If the second head sees you, it snatches you up and takes its time grinding you to a pulp in its powerful jaws. But the third head is the worst. Its fierce glare pierces your very soul, causing such despair you kill yourself.

AMARYLLIS

And that's what wants to catch me?

FEY
What else did you expect in the Land of the Dead?

AMARYLLIS
Why didn't you tell me this before?

FEY
I never said it would be easy.

AMARYLLIS
That's not all you didn't say.

FEY
You're not calling off the mission, are you?

AMARYLLIS
You bet I am! Let's go, princess, we're going home.

In the distance we hear the rending cry of the beast at bay.

FEY
It's too late.

AMARYLLIS
This is a nightmare!

FEY
The dog has picked up your scent.

AMARYLLIS
I want to wake up!

FEY
The forest is just ahead. We can hide there. Let's go!

The two girls run off.

3.

DAD enters.

NARRATOR
Meanwhile, Amaryllis's dad was running all over town. He ran without knowing where to go. Where should he look for her? Which street, which alley, which park? He ran past all the familiar places. He ran, but the empty feeling inside kept growing and growing. He ran, trying not to think. Don't think, don't think, just keep looking, looking, breathe, keep breathing . . .

The phone rings.

DAD
Hello?

NARRATOR
"Mr. Gray?"

DAD
Speaking.

NARRATOR
"Sergeant Baxter here."

DAD
Did you find her?

NARRATOR
"No, not yet."

DAD
I'm worried to death.

NARRATOR
"We're doing everything we can."

DAD
Do you have any leads?

NARRATOR
"That's actually why I'm calling, Mr. Gray. I have a few questions I'd like to ask you, to help with our investigation."

DAD
Please, ask me anything.

NARRATOR
"First: have you noticed anything different about your daughter lately, a change of mood perhaps?"

DAD
No . . .

NARRATOR
"Any new friends?"

DAD
No, none . . .

NARRATOR
"Have you had any disagreements lately?"

DAD
What do you mean, "disagreements"?

NARRATOR
"Discipline problems, an argument, that sort of thing."

DAD
No, I don't see what—

NARRATOR
"The school principal told me that you have custody of your
daughter—"

DAD
Usually her mother and I have joint custody, but she's away at
the moment.

NARRATOR
"Then I have to ask you, Mr. Gray: in your opinion, why would
your daughter decide to run away now?"

DAD
What are you trying to say?

NARRATOR

"Whatever you can tell us at this point would be a huge help."

DAD

I don't understand.

NARRATOR

"Every minute that goes by reduces our chances of finding your daughter."

DAD

Sergeant, my daughter was perfectly fine until this happened. I have no clue why she ran away!

NARRATOR

"In that case, I have no further questions."

DAD

You're going to find her, right?

NARRATOR

"We'll call you as soon as we know anything."

DAD

Wait—!

DAD hangs up the phone and runs off.

4.

At that very moment, the two sisters enter the forest.
AMARYLLIS is holding her nose.

FEY
Hide. Quick!

AMARYLLIS
What stinks so bad?

FEY
It's the forest. Stay close to the trees.

AMARYLLIS
This place smells worse than a garbage dump.

FEY
Exactly. The dog won't pick up your scent in here.

AMARYLLIS
The ground's moving.

FEY
Worms. Hold on to the branches so you don't fall.

AMARYLLIS
Even the trees are rotten!

FEY
They're made of bones. The trunks are tibia, the branches are humerus, and the twigs are fingers.

AMARYLLIS

What are those buds at the tips of the branches?

FEY

Skulls, but they aren't in season.

AMARYLLIS

What do you do with them when they're ripe? Make jam?

FEY

When the skulls ripen, they crash to the ground and rot. You can't eat anything here; everything's poison.

AMARYLLIS

Remind me why I'm here again? Oh, yeah. To save my family. Worst idea ever.

FEY

How can you say that?

AMARYLLIS

Because it's too late. Mom's already left.
New job, new life.

FEY

She still loves him.

AMARYLLIS

How do you know?

FEY

She speaks to me when I go see her in her dreams.

AMARYLLIS
And Dad? What does he say?

FEY
I don't know.

AMARYLLIS
You don't go see him?

FEY
I do, all the time, but he never sees me. His dream is always the same: he's wandering alone in an endless desert.

AMARYLLIS
I'm so not surprised.

FEY
You're very hard on him.

AMARYLLIS
It's not my fault Dad's acting like a doofus.

FEY
He's just sad.

AMARYLLIS
What about me? It's like I don't exist.

FEY
This is all my fault. I shouldn't have brought you here.

AMARYLLIS

You said it was the only way to set you free.

FEY

Exactly! If you untie my ribbon, I'll leave you too.

AMARYLLIS

That's different; I want you to go.

FEY

Why would you say that?

AMARYLLIS

How old are you?

FEY

Nine. Why?

AMARYLLIS

Do you know today's date?

FEY

No.

AMARYLLIS

May 12. What's May 12?

FEY

Your birthday.

AMARYLLIS

Bull's eye. Today, I turn ten.

FEY

So?

AMARYLLIS

So, it means from now on you can't protect me anymore, because I'm older than you. It means I'm going to be a teenager, then an adult, and you're never going to change, and I don't want to feel bad about it for the rest of my life. Don't you get it? I don't want to take your place; I don't want to live for two; I just want to be myself. Do you understand? Fey?

FEY

The dog's gone from view,
the danger has passed,
we can continue
pursuing our quest.

AMARYLLIS

Fey, do you understand?

FEY

Enough said—
the story must unfurl.
Your mission lies ahead.
Let's go kill the dead girl.

FEY exits. AMARYLLIS watches her go, and then exits.

5.

DAD enters at a run. He stops and looks around. The phone rings. He answers.

DAD
Hello?

NARRATOR
"It's Brigid."

DAD
I'm sorry, who?

NARRATOR
"You know, your ex, the mother of your children."

DAD
I can't hear you. You're breaking up.

NARRATOR
"My taxi's driving through a field of sheep. It's pure hell! Philip, the police just called."

DAD
Yeah, I know.

NARRATOR
"What's going on?"

DAD
What's going on? I lost our daughter.

NARRATOR
"When were you planning to tell me?"

DAD
Calm down, Brigid.

NARRATOR
"My daughter's missing and you want me to calm down?"

DAD
Now, now, don't get upset.

NARRATOR
"Where are you?"

DAD
At the house.

NARRATOR
"What are you doing at the house?"

DAD
What do you think? I'm looking for her!

NARRATOR
"Why did she do it, Philip?"

DAD
I don't know.

NARRATOR
"What happened?"

DAD
I don't know.

NARRATOR
"We'll get to the bottom of it. I'm heading to the airport now to catch the first flight out. I'll be there as soon as I can."

DAD
That's not necessary.

NARRATOR
"Let me be the judge of what is or isn't necessary."

DAD
Okay, go on, just say it.

NARRATOR
"Say what?"

DAD
This is all my fault.

NARRATOR
"I would never say that."

DAD
She ran away, just like you did.

NARRATOR
"I didn't run away."

DAD
Yeah, right.

NARRATOR
"I needed to find myself."

DAD
On the other side of the world? I don't get it, Brigid. I did every-thing I could. I'm working like crazy, taking care of everything. Tell me, what more can I do?

NARRATOR
"It's more complicated than that."

DAD
Why do I always end up alone?

NARRATOR
"But that's just it. You're not alone."

DAD
I don't understand what you're trying to say.

NARRATOR
"And that's why she ran away."

DAD
I should keep looking for her instead of talking on the phone.

NARRATOR
"Fine, end of discussion. I'll call you as soon as I know something."

*DAD hangs up. He looks around, then goes to exit. He stops.
He picks up the phone and dials.*

DAD
Hello, Brigid?

NARRATOR
"Sorry?"

DAD
It's Philip, your ex, the one who loses your children.

NARRATOR
"Speak louder. A herd of elephants is blocking the road."

DAD
Do you remember where you wanted to scatter Fey's ashes?

NARRATOR
"What?"

DAD
Did you ever talk to Amaryllis about where you wanted to scatter
the ashes?

NARRATOR
"Maybe once, when we were walking by the pier. I might have
said I'd like the water to carry Fey away, so she could see the
world. Something like that. Why do you ask?"

DAD
The urn's gone.

NARRATOR
"You think Amaryllis took it?"

DAD
I'll call you as soon as I know something.

NARRATOR
"Wait!"

DAD hangs up and runs off.

6.

Crowd sounds. AMARYLLIS enters. She sees a shadow and approaches.

AMARYLLIS
Fey? Fey?

FEY enters.

FEY
I'm here.

AMARYLLIS
Where are we?

FEY
At the garden gates. Where our journey ends.

AMARYLLIS
What's that sound?

FEY
Souls looking for a door.

AMARYLLIS
Are you sure they can't hurt me?

FEY
Trust me. You're in no danger.

The sound of a dog's bark.

AMARYLLIS
You were saying?

FEY
Don't move.

AMARYLLIS
How am I supposed to stay still when something's coming to eat me?

FEY
Sshh! Be quiet.

AMARYLLIS
It's too late, it's too late. I knew it. It's too late!

FEY

No, sister! Run to the gates. The garden lies just beyond.
See the tree on that hill? Just head straight for it.

AMARYLLIS

What are you going to do?

FEY

Protect you for the last time.

AMARYLLIS

Are you sure you can?

FEY

Trust your Super Sister! Now, run! Run as fast as you can, and
don't stop, no matter what!

AMARYLLIS

Roger that.

FEY

Farewell, sister.

AMARYLLIS runs off. FEY confronts the dog (Cerberus).

Easy. Easy. Don't be afraid. Night is watching over me, and
Death will have its way. That's it, easy, easy. There's nothing for
you here.

The NARRATOR enters.

NARRATOR

Amaryllis ran up the hill until she reached the foot of the white tree and raced around its massive trunk. Among the millions of ribbons, she recognized a golden thread fluttering in the breeze and instantly knew that it was the one she'd been searching for all along.

AMARYLLIS stops.

AMARYLLIS

Hey, what are you doing here?

NARRATOR

I'm here to welcome you to my garden.

AMARYLLIS

This is where you live?

NARRATOR

Yes. Actually, I'm the one who planted this tree.

AMARYLLIS

So you're Death?

NARRATOR

You could say that.

AMARYLLIS

Why is Death telling the story?

NARRATOR
Death is an ending. To exist, I need stories. It makes sense, don't you think?

AMARYLLIS
If you say so.

NARRATOR
Well, that's how you made it all the way to the Ribbon Tree.

AMARYLLIS
It was almost too easy.

NARRATOR
Are you going to climb to the top?

AMARYLLIS
Yup. Give me a boost?

NARRATOR
If I touch you, you'll die. Remember who I am.

AMARYLLIS
Forget it. I'll figure it out myself.

AMARYLLIS climbs the tree.

NARRATOR
Are you sure it's the right ribbon?

AMARYLLIS
Yeah, I'm sure.

NARRATOR

How do you know?

AMARYLLIS

Call it women's intuition.

NARRATOR

Oh, is that what it is.

AMARYLLIS

My sister has the same ribbon in her hair. I might be a brat, but I have eyes.

NARRATOR

Isn't it too high for you?

AMARYLLIS

Nah, I'm used to it.

NARRATOR

This won't fix everything, you know. Everyone has to grieve in their own time.

AMARYLLIS

Please be quiet. I can't concentrate.

NARRATOR

Are you sure the branch is strong enough to hold you?

AMARYLLIS

I'm almost there.

NARRATOR

Watch out! It looks like it's about to break.

AMARYLLIS grabs hold of the ribbon.

AMARYLLIS

I've got it!

NARRATOR

And so it came to pass that, unable to support the weight of the living any longer, the branch of the white tree gave way, along with the child, who fell into the darkness and disappeared.

7.

DAD runs on. He stops when he sees AMARYLLIS on the ground. He takes her in his arms.

AMARYLLIS

I don't want to die, I don't want to die . . .

DAD

It's all right . . . it's okay . . . I'm here . . . You're safe now . . .

AMARYLLIS

Daddy? I was so scared.

DAD

What got into you? Why did you run away? What were you thinking? I was worried to death. You want me to drop dead, is that it? Say it: "Dad, I want you to drop dead."

AMARYLLIS

Listen, Dad, let me explain . . .

DAD

No, you listen to me! I've been running all over town, picturing the worst, and for what? For nothing! From now on, no more acting up, got it? No more calls from the principal. No more stunts, no more pranks, no more drama! Understand?

AMARYLLIS *(softly)*

Yes.

DAD

Do you understand?

AMARYLLIS *(louder)*

Yes, Dad, I understand.

DAD

Good! Now, I have to call every single person in the entire city to tell them I found you.

> *DAD picks up the phone just as it starts to ring. He answers. While he's speaking, AMARYLLIS discovers the gold ribbon in her hand.*

Hello?

NARRATOR

"Hello, Philip? It's the office. Where the heck are you?"

DAD
Long story.

NARRATOR
"You know what's long? Waiting for you for the past two hours."

DAD
I'll be there as soon as I can.

NARRATOR
"Your client called. We told him you went out. He wasn't too happy."

DAD
I'll take care of it.

NARRATOR
"Sure, but the question is: When?"

DAD
Later.

NARRATOR
"Later as in now, or later as in later?"

DAD
Later than now. How's that for an answer?

NARRATOR
"Not good. Not good at all, actually. An entire team is waiting for the client's input before they can push ahead. So get your sorry self in here right now and do what we pay you to do."

DAD
I've got to take care of my daughter.

NARRATOR
"Who cares about your daughter?"

DAD
Excuse me?

NARRATOR
"You need to make a choice: What's more important?"

DAD
You're asking me to choose between you and my daughter?

NARRATOR
"Look, if you let us down, you won't get a second chance. People are counting on you. You're jeopardizing their jobs, and for what? Because your daughter got in trouble. Again. The more you coddle her, the more she acts up, the more you run around like a chicken—"

DAD interrupts the NARRATOR by hanging up and stomping on his phone. AMARYLLIS gapes at him.

DAD
All right, then.

AMARYLLIS *(showing him the ribbon)*
Daddy? Could you tie this in my hair?

AMARYLLIS hands DAD the gold ribbon she's been holding onto for dear life.

DAD
Now's not a good time.

AMARYLLIS
What's more important?

DAD takes the ribbon and ties it in AMARYLLIS's hair. FEY appears. The NARRATOR approaches FEY and removes her princess dress. Underneath, she is wearing a hospital gown.

FEY
Daddy . . .

DAD
What?

AMARYLLIS
I didn't say anything.

FEY
Daddy . . .

DAD
So whose voice is that?

Suddenly, DAD sees FEY.

FEY
Daddy, I need you.

DAD
I'm here. I'm taking you home with me. We're all going home together.

FEY
No, Daddy.

DAD
Don't say that.

FEY
I have to go.

DAD
Stay with me.

FEY
I did everything I could.

DAD
We can still fight this.

FEY
I'm tired, Daddy. Please, let me go.

DAD
I can't.

FEY
It's the last thing I'll ever ask you for.

DAD
I can't.

FEY
Let me go.

DAD doesn't move.

AMARYLLIS
Daddy . . . ?

DAD
What . . . ?

AMARYLLIS
What do we do now?

DAD
I don't know.

AMARYLLIS
I do.

AMARYLLIS gives the urn to her DAD.

DAD
What do you want me to do?

AMARYLLIS
Scatter Fey's ashes in the water.

DAD

I can't.

AMARYLLIS

Well, I can't live with Zombie Dad. So you better choose. Or else, one day, I'm going to leave you too!

DAD

You realize if I do this your mother's going to kill me.

AMARYLLIS

Why don't we ask her?

DAD

I guess it wouldn't hurt to try.

> *DAD checks his pockets for his phone.*

Oh, no.

AMARYLLIS

What?

DAD

My phone; I can't call her. Listen, why don't we do this another day, okay? It'll give us time to think everything through, weigh the pros and cons . . .

AMARYLLIS

Wait, I have another idea.

AMARYLLIS turns toward the NARRATOR, who throws her his phone.

Thanks.

She dials.

Hello, Mom? It's me. Huh? What? Yeah, we found each other. I'm fine, great, actually. Where are you?

You don't know?

(to DAD) Her taxi got lost.

(into phone) Yeah, I can't wait to see you too. I've got tons of things to tell you. But first I gotta ask you something a bit strange but super important. Remember that one time when we were walking down by the pier—? Well, for my birthday I want to free Fey. Do you mind if we scatter her ashes in the river? Yeah, I want her to go too.

(to DAD) She said yes.

(into the phone) What? You want to stay on the line? Okay.

AMARYLLIS points the phone at her DAD.

Permission granted.

DAD
So, what now?

AMARYLLIS

Mom's listening.

DAD

I can't believe we're doing this.

AMARYLLIS

Look, I don't how good her phone plan is, but it's probably not unlimited.

DAD

Okay, okay, let's do it . . .

> DAD *advances to the river's edge, opens the urn, and empties it. The* NARRATOR *takes* FEY's *hand.*

AMARYLLIS

Goodbye, little sister.

NARRATOR

And that's how the river's black waters carried the ashes of Amaryllis's sister away on her new journey.

But that is another story.

> *The end.*

Little Witch

To all the resilient souls out there.

Author's Acknowledgements

I would like to express my gratitude to Nini Bélanger, Elizabeth Bourget, Paul Lefebvre, and Suzanne Lebeau, who guided me through the writing process. I would also like to thank Emmanuelle Lussier-Martinez, Catherine-Amélie Côté, Gaétan Nadeau, and Dany Boudreault for their generosity. And a nod to Mario Mercier who, unbeknownst to him, sparked this tale.

Translator's Acknowledgements

Pascal Brullemans and I would like to acknowledge the support of the 2017 Banff Playwrights Lab, under director Brian Quirt, and the faith and vision of Geordie Theatre's artistic director, Mike Payette. We would also like to thank the following for their contributions, made during the translation workshop held by Geordie Theatre in spring 2018: dramaturg/director Arianna Bardesono and performers Mike Hughes, Julie Tamiko Manning, and Mike Payette. To Nini Bélanger and Emmanuelle Lussier-Martinez, we profess our gratitude for their invaluable assistance finalizing the text for international performance and publication.

Last but not least, the translator would like to express her gratitude to the author for entrusting her with this little treasure.

Author's Preface

This story's heroine is a child who is shy but who listens. As I wrote, it became clear to me that only a storytelling style would do. In hindsight, I realized that this approach was also ideal for addressing certain questions with the requisite distance. Fairy tales can describe the most tragic circumstances while enabling the hero—or heroine—to change the course of his or her own destiny. By writing this tale, I wanted to let children know that it was possible to escape the monsters, but that triumphing over them would require great determination; it was perfectly normal to feel scared. *Little Witch*'s world consists of silences and enigmas. The silences leave a great deal of room for interpretation, which is why I chose to leave the dialogue unassigned. The story can be told by each character in turn, leaving the reader free to decide how best to apportion the text.

Enjoy.

Translator's Foreword

What I love about this play is that it is about words. How words make something from nothing, shape us and the world around us, make us but also break us. How if we listen very carefully to the words lobbed at us like stones, we can turn them into butterflies. Or bread sticks. Or biscuits. Or a road to carry us away.

What I love about this play is that it is about stories. How stories sustain us, guide us, and how even when we outgrow (or are forced to outgrow) one story, there is always another story waiting to find us and guide us someplace else.

What I love about this play is that it is about courage, even when that courage seems so hard to find. Sometimes, to survive, we have to face what we fear the most and let go of what we love the most and brave the unknown.

Last but not least, this play is about love. The love of words and of stories, the love we have and the love we find, the love we feel for ourselves and for each other.

Petite Sorcière was first produced by Projet MÛ at Théâtre Aux Écuries, Montréal, in November 2017 with the following cast and creative team:

Catherine Allard
Dany Boudreault
Emmanuelle Lussier-Martinez
Gaétan Nadeau

Director: Nini Bélanger
Assistant Director: Chloé Ekker
Set Design: Patrice Charbonneau-Brunelle
Costume Design: Marilène Bastien
Lighting Design: David-Alexandre Chabot
Sound Design: Mathieu Doyon
Video Design: Antonin Gougeon / HUB Studio
Technical Director: Jérémi Guilbault-Asselin
Production Manager: Maude St-Pierre

The English translation of *Petite Sorcière* was developed with the support of the 2017 Banff Playwrights Lab under director Brian Quirt, and commissioned by Geordie Theatre under artistic director Mike Payette.

Little Witch was first produced for Geordie Theatre's 2018–19 2Play School Tour, touring to Quebec, Ontario, and the Maritimes with the following cast and creative team:

Skyler Clark
Qianna MacGilchrist
Lex Roy

Director: Arianna Bardesono
Costume Design: Diana Uribe
Sound Design: Rob Denton
Prop Design: Mathieu Cardin
Lighting Design: Tim Rodrigues
Production Manager: Amy-Susie Bradford

Characters

Little Witch
Big Witch
Hunter Boy
The ogre

Settings

Apartment
Shack
Forest
Palace

1.

Little Witch lives in the city with her mother Big Witch
Big Witch is very sick and has to lie down a lot

When her mother is too tired to stir
Little Witch takes care of her
Washing the dishes and tending the herbs

2.

Little Witch likes to go to the mall
To listen to the sounds of daily life
Ringing out like an orchestra
In a humungous concert hall

But the people who see her pass by
Dirty and poorly dressed
Roll their eyes and say
What a grubby little girl!
Her mother must be a witch

Little Witch goes home
Arms full of groceries
Mouth crammed with really bad words

Her mother overhears and bursts out laughing

BIG WITCH

People are idiots
I'm so glad to be a witch
For I see more than meets the eye
I know my girl is truly beautiful

Little Witch replies that she is glad to be a witch too

3.

Big Witch goes to see the doctors
who prescribe a heap of remedies
But Big Witch doesn't improve
One morning she gets out of bed and says

BIG WITCH

All doctors are cretins
I'm so glad to be a witch
For I'm so clever and the best problem solver
Now I've heard tell a quick way to get well
Before dawn a magic flower must I gather
that grows in the deep dark wood
But it can only be found by witches who possess
two special qualities
A fire in their belly and wings on their feet

Little Witch replies that her belly and wings are HUGE

4.

The witches pack their bags
and leave the city, heading for the woods
But their bags are too heavy and hurt their arms
Big Witch tosses those bags in the ditch and says

BIG WITCH
Why keep so many useless things?
I'm so glad to be a witch
For I'm free and don't need a thing

This time Little Witch has no reply

5.

After walking for a long long time
The two witches reach the forest
Luckily, Big Witch finds shelter
A damp dark shack
Little Witch would like to go back
But Big Witch grabs a broom and says

BIG WITCH
Once it's clean
It will be better than a palace

Little Witch replies that she's never seen a palace
But she doesn't think this place measures up
Suddenly she hears a nearby
Crack

Uneasy Little Witch goes into the shack
Without seeing the boy watching her
Hidden on the path

HUNTER BOY
I saw the witch and her daughter
Come up the other road
No food, no nothing
Like two ghosts
I live with Grandfather
In the village on the edge of the forest
Grandfather used to be a hunter
So he taught me how to find my way
hunt for food and hide it
Surviving here
Takes smarts

6.

In the shack
Little Witch takes a rag to combat the cockroaches and centipedes
Suddenly she hears purring near the fireplace
A cat is sleeping on the blackened stones
Looking over her shoulder Big Witch shrugs and says

BIG WITCH
Looks like you found a friend
I'm so glad to be a witch
For my instincts always lead me to the right place
so good things can happen

Little Witch likes her new home
Even though it is dark and smelly

7.

Little Witch and the cat go out to explore
The forest is alive with strange and mysterious sounds
Little Witch listens . . . more

LITTLE WITCH
A bird pecks a tree
Drops plop on leaves
Twigs snap underfoot

The cat shows her how to skip from rock to rock without falling
into the stream
Together, they fill a basket with nice big mushrooms
But at the edge of the path the cat stops
Little Witch hides
She sees a boy walking through the woods
At that very moment, a clumsy toad falls into the water

Kerplunk

Little Witch turns back around
But the boy has disappeared

8.

When night falls over the forest
Big Witch lights a fire
takes her basket and says

> BIG WITCH
> Tonight I will look for the magic flower
> Stay here and don't let anyone in

Little Witch watches her mother disappear
Then shuts the door
Picks up the old blanket
Huddles in the armchair by the fire
The cat asleep on her lap

The night wears on
Little Witch hears the wind moaning through the branches
The owl chasing the field mice on the roof
Little Witch shivers
But she just can't sleep

When the sky turns peach
Big Witch reappears on the path
Back bowed by fatigue
Basket still empty

9.

One day, Big Witch asks her daughter to fetch some water
When Little Witch gets to the stream
She sees the boy from the path sitting on a rock
He is skipping stones and watching them ricochet

> HUNTER BOY
> You're the witch's daughter

Little Witch finds him very rude
She fills her pail without replying
But the boy stops her

> HUNTER BOY
> Grandfather says your mother came here
> to find a magic flower
> to make some witchy potions
> But she won't find it

Little Witch asks why not

> HUNTER BOY
> Grandfather says
> Only the eyes of a child can see the magic flower in the forest at night
> Grandfather also says it's clear your mother is from the city
> The only thing she's good at is getting lost in the woods
> I've known this forest since I was this high
> If your mother pays me I'll find the flower for her

Little Witch replies that witches don't have any money

HUNTER BOY
That's too bad
I'll just keep the flower for myself
to sell at the mall
Then I'll be rich as a king

Little Witch replies that she'd rather be a witch
then heads back to the shack
cat at her heels

10.

Night falls once again over the forest
Big Witch puts on her coat
Picks up her basket
But her legs shake

Little Witch takes her hand
to guide her along the path

Too weak to protest
Big Witch lets herself be led

11.

Despite the dark
Little Witch marches on
But Big Witch falls behind

> **LITTLE WITCH**
> Hurry up, Mom!
> The sun will soon be up

> **BIG WITCH**
> Let's stop for a minute

> **LITTLE WITCH**
> What is it?

> **BIG WITCH**
> You know the life of a witch
> is not always easy
> But at least I chose it freely

> **LITTLE WITCH**
> That's all that counts

> **BIG WITCH**
> Yes . . .
> No
> You're all that counts
> You are the light of my life

> **LITTLE WITCH**
> I love you too, Mom

Suddenly a howl cracks the air
Petrified Little Witch hides behind a tree
Watches her mother head off

BIG WITCH
Wait here

Big Witch disappears down the path
Leaving her daughter all alone
Amid the sounds of the deep dark wood

12.

In a clearing
Big Witch discovers an ogre
Lying on a carpet of leaves
His foot caught in a trap

OGRE
What are you looking at?

BIG WITCH
A dying monster
This forest is just full of surprises

OGRE
I know the hunter who did this
He was lucky to get away from me

BIG WITCH
He certainly won't return the favour

OGRE

Like you're any better

BIG WITCH

What do you mean?

OGRE

If I were human you'd set me free

BIG WITCH

You're wrong
I am a witch
Humans or monsters
They're all the same

OGRE

Oh there's a difference

BIG WITCH

Is there?

OGRE

Ogres always keep their word
Otherwise they die
It's the law

BIG WITCH

What law?

OGRE

The law in the kingdom of the fairies

BIG WITCH
So what?

OGRE
Think, Witch
If we strike a deal
My promise is your guarantee—
Just set me free

BIG WITCH
In that case you're as good as freed
If you tell me
Where to find the magic flower
That grows in the deep dark wood

OGRE
Sorry, Witch
There's no such flower
The ogres spread this rumour
To draw children to the wood

Big Witch shuts her eyes
A wave of exhaustion crashes over her

OGRE
I'm not the only one to die tonight
Your life is slipping away like rice from a ripped bag

BIG WITCH
I want to change the terms of our deal
I'll set you free but in exchange
Swear to keep my daughter
When I die

OGRE
You want to give your daughter to an ogre?

BIG WITCH
You will not harm her

OGRE
I can't keep a child!

BIG WITCH
So no deal?

OGRE
You're crazy!

BIG WITCH
In that case . . .

OGRE
Wait!
I swear to keep your daughter when you die
Okay? Satisfied?

BIG WITCH
It's a deal

Big Witch opens the trap
The iron jaws release their grasp
Free, the ogre rises up like a mountain

BIG WITCH
I kept my part of the deal

OGRE
And I'll keep mine
So long, Witch

Retracing her steps
Big Witch finds her little girl
Trembling and terrified
She takes her child in her arms
Hugs her so tight and says

BIG WITCH
Time to go back

LITTLE WITCH
What about the magic flower?

BIG WITCH
We'll look for it another time

13.

By the time they get back to the shack
day has dawned
Completely worn out
Big Witch collapses into bed
Little Witch makes a fire to heat the soup
sits in the armchair
cuddles the cat on her lap
waits for her mother to wake up
But she doesn't

Not that day
Or the next
Or the day after that
Or ever again

14.

The fire is out
The cat scratches at her dish
Little Witch shivers with cold
Three knocks at the door

Bam bam bam!

It is the ogre

OGRE
What's your name?

LITTLE WITCH
Little Witch

OGRE
Know who I am?

LITTLE WITCH
You are the ogre

OGRE
Enough with the introductions
Get your things and come

LITTLE WITCH
Where are you taking me?

OGRE
My place

LITTLE WITCH
Are you going to eat me?

OGRE
I promised your mother I'd look after you
I don't have any choice but to keep you
Here we are

LITTLE WITCH
Where?

OGRE
My place

Obeying his orders
the forest pulls back
to reveal an avenue leading to a castle

LITTLE WITCH
Oh, it looks like a . . . palace

OGRE
I wanted something a little more modern
But the workers charged a fortune
So I ate them
Your room's upstairs
If you're hungry
I left a savoury pie on the dresser

LITTLE WITCH
Thank you

OGRE
I also put a clock in there
It's better if we don't see each other
I usually go out about midnight
Come back before sunrise
So that's when you should eat and wash
After that go back up to your room
and lock yourself in
Here's the key
Don't lose it
I got rid of the spare
Too risky
Okay gotta go
See you

Alone in the room
Little Witch looks out the small window
A single ray of light is dying between the trees
She strokes the satin quilt on the canopy bed
Missing most terribly
The cold shack in the deep dark wood

15.

The clock chimes
Little Witch wakes up
Looks around
The bed, the room
And shuts her eyes

Opens them
Shuts them
Opens them
Shuts them
Opens them
Sits up
Sighs
Gets up

She glances out the window
at the night quiet and calm
Walks around the room
Once
Twice
Jumps on the bed
Messes up the sheets

Climbs up the curtains
Scratches the carpet
Looks through the keyhole
Picks up the key
Puts down the key
Picks up the key
Puts down the key
Picks up the key
In the keyhole
Turns the lock
Opens the door

In the hall
She creeps along the wall
Like a cat
Passes by a mirror

> LITTLE WITCH
> Circles around the eyes
> Mop of dark hair
> Yes
> That's me

She walks down the stairs without a creak
Discovers gardens filled with sweet-smelling flowers
Explores nooks and crannies full of rare and precious objects

> LITTLE WITCH
> Why keep so many useless things?

Little Witch stops and listens . . . more
But she hears nothing
No wind, no rain, no people, no life
Nothing

She continues on to the end of the hall
Toward the ogre's room
She knows she is not supposed to
That it would be better to go back
But she goes in anyway
And sees
She sees

> OGRE
> What are you doing here?

> LITTLE WITCH
> Nothing

> OGRE
> You shouldn't be out and about at this hour!

> LITTLE WITCH
> I'm sorry

> OGRE
> Go to your room!

Little Witch goes to her room
Shuts the door
Forgets to lock it

16.

Ignoring the child
The ogre returns to his ogre life
Sleeping by day, hunting by night
But when he gets home
The monster finds that the child's odour
Sweet and addictive
Whets his appetite
Plagues his sleep
Wrings him out, lays him low
Like a sickness

But one morning
As he is returning to the palace
Tired and starving as usual
The monster smells a different smell in the hall
That reminds him of wilted flowers
Worried, he crosses the gardens
Tears up the stairs
to the bedroom
Knocks on the door
No answer
Turns the knob
The door opens

The child is there
Stretched out on the bed
Eyes shut
Still
Pale
Skinny as a rail

Her breath barely a tremble
She is letting herself die

The ogre has no choice
If the child dies his fate is sealed
He leans over her
takes her gently in his arms
and carries her to the kitchen

17.

Little Witch sits before a sumptuous feast
Across the table
The ogre watches her

>OGRE
>You don't like it?

>LITTLE WITCH
>Looks delicious

>OGRE
>So eat

Little Witch doesn't budge

>OGRE
>You have to eat
>I order you to eat!
>If you don't eat I'll—

LITTLE WITCH
Do what?
What could be worse
than being here with you?

OGRE
What do you want?

LITTLE WITCH
My mother

OGRE
Sorry for your loss
But she chose her fate
You can make another choice

LITTLE WITCH
I would like to have my cat

OGRE
Take a bite
And I'll go get it

LITTLE WITCH
You mean it?

OGRE
I always keep my word

Little Witch picks up her fork and eats

OGRE
It's a deal
So . . . is it good?

Little Witch replies that she has never eaten anything so—

OGRE
Stop saying that!

LITTLE WITCH
What did I say?

OGRE
Little Witch this and Little Witch that

LITTLE WITCH
It's my name

OGRE
As of now your name is the same as mine
Understood?

LITTLE WITCH
Understood

Beat.

LITTLE WITCH
If my name is yours
It's like I'm your daughter
Sort of like we're family

OGRE
Yes
Sort of
Now we're bound together

18.

The next day
Little . . .
          Ogre opens her eyes
To find the cat next to her on the bed
Yawning and stretching like a lion
Ready to take on the world

Overjoyed she dances around the room with the cat
Telling her stories and combing her fur
But something catches her attention
On the dresser next to the clock
A crown

LITTLE WITCH
Fits me like a glove

Time ticks by
The hungry cat jumps off the bed
and stands by the door mewing
Little Ogre looks at the clock

LITTLE WITCH
We'll go out later tonight

She picks up her friend
and strokes the cat's back, smiling

19.

Midnight chimes
Little Ogre and the cat go out to explore
Pass by the mirror in the hall

> **LITTLE WITCH**
> With the crown
> I totally look like someone else

More practical
The cat passes by nooks and crannies and gardens and heads
    straight for the kitchen
The copper pots hanging above the ovens
The cupboards full of crockery and canisters
The humungous table and ebony counters
Where armies of silver utensils slumber

Little Ogre fills a dish and sets it down
Then she sits by the cat, who pounces on her meal

> **LITTLE WITCH**
> Do you think we can live here?
> Obviously it's not perfect
> But at least it's warm
> The food's good
> The bed's comfy

That's already quite a lot
Maybe I can learn to live
Like an ogre

20.

The days pass by
Little Ogre and the cat often go out
Running in the halls
Gliding along the floors
Diving into pillows

Criss-crossing the gardens and making bouquets
Little Ogre finds a flower in a vase
Bigger and more colourful than all the other flowers

OGRE
I know what you're thinking
But you're wrong
Magic flowers—no such thing

LITTLE WITCH
Maybe you don't have enough imagination

OGRE
It's one of the only faults that ogres don't have

LITTLE WITCH
You aren't going out?

OGRE
Tonight?
No need

LITTLE WITCH
Why's that?

OGRE
I have everything right here

Little Ogre picks up her cat
and goes back to her room
But before she can lock the door
She hears a noise
Stills and listens . . . more

Searching for the source of the sound
Little Ogre goes to the kitchen
Approaches the cupboard
Sees the padlock

HUNTER BOY
Who's there?

She recognizes the voice
It is the boy from the path

LITTLE WITCH
It's me
The witch's daughter

HUNTER BOY
Grandfather thought you were dead

LITTLE WITCH
Why are you here?

HUNTER BOY
Because of you
The story of the flower
I wanted so badly to find it
That I kept looking
Further and further away
Closer and closer to the place
Grandfather said I should never go
And I got caught

LITTLE WITCH
That was dumb

HUNTER BOY
Can you get me out of here?

LITTLE WITCH
The ogre padlocked the door

HUNTER BOY
Where's the key?

LITTLE WITCH
I don't know

HUNTER BOY
So I'm going to die

LITTLE WITCH
I'm so sorry

The boy starts to cry again
Little Ogre runs out of the kitchen
Hands over her ears

21.

Running through the palace
Little Ogre climbs the stairs
Passes by the mirror
Turns the corner
Right into the ogre

OGRE
Looks like you've been crying

LITTLE WITCH
Doesn't matter

OGRE
Because of the cat?

LITTLE WITCH
Because of the boy

OGRE

You shouldn't have talked to him

LITTLE WITCH

Are you really going to eat a kid?

OGRE

It's my nature

LITTLE WITCH

You can't change?

OGRE

I will always be an ogre

LITTLE WITCH

I can't let you do it

OGRE

You care that much?

LITTLE WITCH

Yes!

OGRE

So make me a deal

LITTLE WITCH

How?

OGRE
Offer me something in exchange for the boy
And I promise to spare him

LITTLE WITCH
In exchange for the boy
I could give you . . .

OGRE
What do you have?

LITTLE WITCH
Nothing

OGRE
Think

LITTLE WITCH
I could give you
My crown?

OGRE
Already got one

LITTLE WITCH
I could give you
Not my cat!

OGRE
I'm allergic anyway
Tasted one once
Almost suffocated to death

LITTLE WITCH
I could give you
Me?

The monster grins

OGRE
Is it a deal?

LITTLE WITCH
I don't know

OGRE
To make a deal
Both sides have to agree

LITTLE WITCH
I have to think about it

OGRE
I'm very hungry

LITTLE WITCH
Give me time!

OGRE
You've got till tomorrow
When midnight strikes
You will choose
Who I'm having for dinner

22.

In her room
Little Ogre . . .
The little girl
Locks the door
Looks out the window
Sees dawn sketch the treetops
Asking herself what would her mother say?

BIG WITCH
Monsters are always two-faced
They can't be trusted
I'm so glad to be a witch
For I'm so clever and the best problem solver

LITTLE WITCH
I'm not like you, Mom

BIG WITCH
Ogre or witch you'll always be my daughter
Save yourself
Forget the boy

LITTLE WITCH
It would be monstrous

BIG WITCH
At least you'd live

LITTLE WITCH
Not if it means turning into an ogre

BIG WITCH
Got another solution?

The little girl looks out the window

LITTLE WITCH
I could run away

BIG WITCH
You don't run fast enough
He'll just catch you again

The little girl looks at the clock

LITTLE WITCH
I could hit him over the head

BIG WITCH
Too risky
You're not strong enough

The little girl looks at the cat

LITTLE WITCH
No . . .

BIG WITCH
Got another solution?

LITTLE WITCH
No, Mom, I can't do it!

BIG WITCH
What you can't do
is die
So you're going to act like a witch
Follow your instincts and do what you have to do
to survive
Understand?

LITTLE WITCH
No!

BIG WITCH
Don't be a fool
You know I'm right

On her bed
The little girl sobs so hard
That she falls asleep before all her tears have been shed
The cat nestled by her head

23.

The next day
The little girl stays in her room
Even though the cat is starving
Unfortunately midnight strikes
Footsteps on the stairs
Time has run out

OGRE
You've made your choice?

LITTLE WITCH
Yes

OGRE
Who am I having for dinner?

LITTLE WITCH
Me

OGRE
You're sure?

LITTLE WITCH
Absolutely

OGRE
Make me a deal

LITTLE WITCH
If you let me free the boy from the path
I'll break the deal you made with my mother
You won't have to keep me alive anymore

OGRE
You have to free him tonight

LITTLE WITCH
I promise

OGRE
Then it's a deal

LITTLE WITCH
Could I have the key to the cupboard?

OGRE
Only if you give me the key to your room

LITTLE WITCH
Why?

OGRE
You don't need it anymore

The ogre and the child exchange keys

OGRE
Free the prisoner before daybreak
If you break your promise
The deal is off
And I will eat you both

24.

In her bedroom
The little girl can't stop shaking
as she picks up the cat

LITTLE WITCH
Forgive me

In one swift
Crack
She breaks the cat's neck

For one long moment
The child strokes the animal
Lying still on the quilt

25.

The little girl puts the cat in a bag
Snatches the key to the cupboard
Rushes down the stairs
Skirts the gardens
Flies by the nooks and crannies
Enters the kitchen
Lights the oven
Breaks some eggs
Mixes in milk and flour
Empties the bag onto a pie plate
Covers the plate with dough
Puts the plate into the oven
Waits
A moment later
The starving ogre calls out

OGRE
Has the boy been freed?

LITTLE WITCH
Not yet

OGRE
What are you waiting for?

She opens the oven
The dough is still raw

LITTLE WITCH
Just a few minutes more

OGRE
Day is about to break

LITTLE WITCH
Not much longer now

Time ticks by
The ogre is losing patience

OGRE
Free the boy!

The little girl takes the plate out of the oven
Then runs to the cupboard
Turns the key in the lock
The boy from the path is inside
Still very much alive

LITTLE WITCH
Run away now
Go

HUNTER BOY
Come with me

LITTLE WITCH
Not yet

HUNTER BOY
He'll eat you

LITTLE WITCH
Wait for me in the forest
If day breaks and I don't make it
Go back to your grandfather's
Promise to wait for me?

The boy promises and runs off
Just then
The ogre appears

OGRE
Where's the boy?

LITTLE WITCH
He's gone free

OGRE
Time to eat

The girl picks up the plate
Slides it under his nose

LITTLE WITCH
Before I die I would like to serve you this savoury pie
To thank you for taking care of me
Be careful
It's piping hot

Ignoring her warnings
The ogre grabs the pie
Gulps it down in a single bite

LITTLE WITCH
Was it good?

OGRE
A bit bland

LITTLE WITCH
I'm glad

OGRE
The next course will be much tastier

But he stops
Leans on the table
Trying to catch his breath

LITTLE WITCH
Don't feel well?

OGRE
My throat is on fire

LITTLE WITCH
Your face is blue

OGRE
It's like—

LITTLE WITCH
—a cat got your tongue?

OGRE
What did you put in that pie?

LITTLE WITCH
Everything I loved!

Knocking the table over
The ogre collapses

LITTLE WITCH
You will always be an ogre
I will always be a witch

Little Witch listens to the monster suffocate
His heavy, laboured breathing
Whittles down to whistling
Then a few gasps
Then nothing

26.

HUNTER BOY
Hidden in the forest
I saw the witch's daughter come out the door
Like nothing had happened
Where's the child eater?

LITTLE WITCH
He's dead

HUNTER BOY
I didn't know that witches could kill ogres

LITTLE WITCH
Me neither

HUNTER BOY
That's quite a feat
Everyone will fear and respect you
Maybe even write songs about you

LITTLE WITCH
I doubt it

HUNTER BOY
For sure

LITTLE WITCH
In the meantime I'm cold
Can you get us out of this forest?

HUNTER BOY
I brought the witch's daughter to the edge of the woods
Along the road leading to my village
But she stopped
So I said
You saved my life
Even if you are a witch
Grandfather will let you stay
Want to come live with us?

LITTLE WITCH
No

HUNTER BOY
You'd rather go back to your shack?

LITTLE WITCH
Not that either

HUNTER BOY
What do you want to do?

LITTLE WITCH
Follow my instincts
Find the right place

HUNTER BOY
To do what?

LITTLE WITCH
Wait for good things to happen

HUNTER BOY
That might take a while

LITTLE WITCH
Maybe

HUNTER BOY
Will you come back one day?

LITTLE WITCH
I don't know

HUNTER BOY
I'll wait for you anyway

LITTLE WITCH
Thank you

HUNTER BOY
The witch's daughter went down the other road without looking back
Grandfather says she must have gone back to the city
But I know she followed her instincts
And found the right place
To live happily
As a witch

Acknowledgements

Our thanks to Emma Tibaldo and Jessie Mill for bringing us back together.

Pascal Brullemans got into the National Theatre School to woo a girl, only to discover that he actually had talent; his first play was directed by Wajdi Mouawad. After a foray into writing for young audiences with *L'armoire*, Pascal reached out to teens with his plays *Isberg* and *Monstres*. *Amaryllis* took top honours at Lyon Playwrights' Days and won the Louise-LaHaye Award for Young Audiences in 2013. He lives in Montréal.

Alexis Diamond is a Montréal-based theatre artist and translator. Her award-winning plays, operas, and translations have been presented across Canada and internationally. Alexis's 2018/19 season included a piece for the Calgary Philharmonic Orchestra and the touring production of *Little Witch*. Her translation of Erika Tremblay-Roy's *The Problem with Pink* was published by Lansman Editeur in fall 2019.

First edition: June 2020
Printed and bound in Canada by Imprimerie Gauvin, Gatineau

Jacket photo by Jérémie Battaglia
Author photo © Christophe Pean
Translator photo © Ron Diamond

**PLAYWRIGHTS
CANADA PRESS**
202-269 Richmond St. W.
Toronto, ON
M5V 1X1

416.703.0013
info@playwrightscanada.com
www.playwrightscanada.com
@playcanpress